The Gate and the

The Gat

by
Dale Roosendaal

The Gate and the Counterfeit

Autograph

The Gate and the Counterfeit

The Gate and the Counterfeit Copyright © 2025 by Dale J. Roosendaal All rights reserved. No part of this book may be reproduced, stored in a retrieval system, or transmitted in any form or by any means—electronic, mechanical, photocopying, recording, or otherwise—without prior written permission of the author, except for brief quotations in reviews or scholarly works. Scripture quotations are from the Holy Bible, ESV® (English Standard Version), copyright © 2001 by Crossway, a publishing ministry of Good News Publishers. Used by permission. All rights reserved and printed in the United States of America.

Editing by Dr. Wanda Berry, Founder of Sovereign Lights Coaching & Mentoring Services, LLC.

Dedication

To my wife Connie, for always believing in me and loving me. Your faith, encouragement, and love have been the anchor that carried this work to completion.

Acknowledgments

I want to thank everyone who supported me through prayer, encouragement, and guidance while I was writing this book. Most importantly, I thank God for His wisdom and grace that made this possible.

The Gate and the Counterfeit

Contents

Foreword 1

Introduction 4

Chapter 1: The Shepherd and the Gate 3

Chapter 2: Born of a Woman: The Divine Entry Point 11

Chapter 3: He Passed Through First Baptism: 17
Threshold, and the Counterfeit Rite

Chapter 4: The Counterfeit Entry 23

The Warning of Jesus 23

Chapter 5: Empty Vessels and Synthetic Life 28

Chapter 6: Satanic Possession: Intrusion, Not 34

Incarnation 34

Chapter 7: The Third Day Gate: Between Resurrection and Rebellion 39

Chapter 8: The False Resurrection: A Counterfeit Triumph 45

Chapter 9: The Image of the Beast: A Counterfeit Presence 50

Chapter 10: The Temple, the Gate, and the Abomination of Desolation 55

Chapter 11: The Mark of the Beast: A Counterfeit Seal 60

Chapter 12: Counterfeit Signs and Wonders: 65

The Gate and the Counterfeit

Deception Masquerading as Power 65

Chapter 13: The Return of the King: The True 70

Gate Revealed 70

Chapter 14: The Return of the King: The True Gate Revealed 74

Chapter 15: The Final Gate: Tomb as Womb 78

The Gate and the Counterfeit

Foreword

In an era when technology outpaces theology and synthetic life begins to blur the boundaries of creation, we must ask more profound questions—questions that pierce beyond doctrine and into the heart of spiritual legitimacy.

This book was born from one such question: What if the "gate" in John 10 is more than a metaphor for salvation? What if it represents the only authorized entry into humanity itself—being born of a woman, as Christ was?

This idea is not commonly taught. It's not found in seminary textbooks or Sunday sermons. Yet it carries profound implications for how we understand the Incarnation, the Antichrist, and the nature of spiritual authority. If Jesus entered through the gate—through birth, prophecy, and divine calling—then any figure who bypasses that gate must be a thief. And if that figure is the Antichrist, then his arrival may not be merely political or charismatic in nature. It may be a

The Gate and the Counterfeit

synthetic, engineered, and spiritually vacant vessel prepared not for redemption, but for possession.

This book explores that possibility with reverence, boldness, and prophetic clarity. It does not claim to have all the answers, but it dares to ask the questions that matter. It traces the gate metaphor through Scripture, contrasts Christ's legitimate entry with the Antichrist's counterfeit climb, and examines how cloning, AI, and false resurrection may play a role in end-time deception.

If you've ever sensed that the world is preparing for something more than just political upheaval—if you've felt that prophecy is unfolding not just in pulpits but in laboratories—then this book is for you. It's a call to discernment, a defense of divine legitimacy, and a reminder that the gate still stands.

Enter through it.

Dale Roosendaal

Introduction

The Gate is a bold and original theological work that reframes John 10 not merely as a metaphor for salvation, but as the exclusive and divinely sanctioned entry into humanity itself.

Rooted in scripture, prophecy, and speculative insight, this book explores the Incarnation as the lawful passage of Christ into the human story—"born of a woman, born under the law"—and draws a striking parallel to the believer's rebirth through the same gate.

Unlike traditional theological texts that treat birth and rebirth as separate doctrines, The Gate unifies them under a single divine principle: legitimacy.

It challenges counterfeit authority, exposes illegitimate spiritual claims, and affirms that proper access to the Kingdom must mirror Christ's own entry—through suffering, obedience, and divine timing.

The Gate and the Counterfeit

This book is not a commentary. It is a filter. A lens. A call to recognize the gate not only as a passage, but as a Person—one who separates the shepherd from the thief, the true from the false, the born from the manifested.

The Gate and the Counterfeit

Chapter 1: The Shepherd and the Gate

At dusk in ancient Israel, the sheepfold stood as a quiet fortress. Stone walls formed a circle of safety, and at its single gate, the watchman kept guard. No stranger could slip in unnoticed. The rightful shepherd entered openly by the gate. Anyone scaling the wall revealed himself as an intruder.

Legitimacy was measured not by words but by how one entered. "Truly, truly, I say to you, he who does not enter the sheepfold by the door but climbs in another way, that man is a thief and a robber" (John 10:1). Then He makes the image startlingly personal: "I am the door of the sheep… I am the good shepherd." The two metaphors overlap. As Shepherd, He leads, provides, and protects. As the Door, He is both the rightful entrant and the very passageway through which life is found. He is at once a model and a mediator, an authority and an access point.

Christ's Legitimate Entry

The Gate and the Counterfeit

Here, the contrast with Antichrist comes into focus. Christ entered rightly — through the gate of God's design. He was born of a woman, submitted to death, and raised by the Spirit. His legitimacy rests on the womb, the tomb, and the resurrection. The Antichrist will bypass these divine thresholds. However dazzling his signs, his very origin betrays him: counterfeit, unauthorized, illegitimate. He is the thief who climbs in another way.

This is no small detail — it reveals the very order of God's kingdom. The Son did not appear in splendor apart from weakness. He did not sidestep death to display resurrection. He entered every boundary of humanity — hunger, grief, frailty, suffering — so that redemption might reach every depth of human life. Authority in God's kingdom comes through submission, not shortcuts. The Antichrist will embody the opposite: take without permission, grasp without surrender, claim without legitimacy.

Scars or Masks?

The Gate and the Counterfeit

    The distinction is not merely metaphorical — it is the measure of authenticity. Christ's authority flows from obedience to the Father's will, sealed in incarnation, cross, and resurrection. The Antichrist's influence will rest on defiance, not sending but intrusion, not life but destruction. One enters by the gate, the other climbs the wall. One lays down His life for the sheep, the other comes only to steal, kill, and destroy. One bears scars; the other wears masks.

Application for Today

    The danger of counterfeit leadership is not confined to the last days. Every generation faces thieves who climb in another way. Some come clothed in religion but are driven by ambition. Others use charisma, manipulation, or even spiritual gifts to seize authority without ever entering through Christ. The question remains: By what gate did they come? True shepherds are tested by their willingness to serve, to submit, and even to suffer. Counterfeits reveal themselves in their hunger for power, platform, and control. For the church, the measure of legitimacy must never be outward success or signs of power, but the path of entry. Was it through obedience, humility, and the Spirit's leading? Or was it by climbing over the wall of self-promotion and spiritual shortcuts?

A Living Illustration

A pastor once described how, when visiting Israel, he watched two shepherds bring their flocks to a single watering hole. The sheep intermingled until they were indistinguishable from one another. But when one shepherd gave his unique call, his sheep immediately separated from the mass and followed. The other shepherd called next, and his sheep gathered to him. No mark on the wool, no branding iron was needed. The sheep knew their shepherd's voice. So, it is with Christ's people. Outward badges of religion do not identify them, but by their responsiveness to His call. The Antichrist may mimic the gestures of a shepherd, but he cannot reproduce the voice.

Reflection & Discussion Questions

The Gate and the Counterfeit

- How does Christ's "entry through the gate" model the true path of authority?
- What modern examples can you think of where leaders have "climbed the wall" instead of entering rightly?
- Why is suffering and obedience such an essential test of legitimacy in God's kingdom?
- In your own walk, how do you discern the Shepherd's voice above competing voices?
- What does it mean for the church to prize scars over masks in leadership?

Prayer Practice

Take a few quiet minutes to imagine the sheepfold. Picture Christ as both Shepherd and Door. Hear His voice calling your name. Ask Him to make His voice more recognizable than all others, and to guard you from those who climb the wall. Prayer: Lord Jesus, Gate of the sheepfold and Shepherd of my soul, teach me to know Your voice. Protect me from thieves who come to steal, kill, and destroy. Help me walk in

The Gate and the Counterfeit

obedience, trusting that Your scars are my life, and Your way is my only gate to the Father. Amen.

Chapter 2: Born of a Woman: The Divine Entry Point

The Humble Threshold of Incarnation

In Galatians 4:4, Paul writes: "When the fullness of time had come, God sent forth His Son, born of a woman, born under the law, to redeem those who were under the law." With deliberate simplicity, the apostle places the most astonishing event in human history within the ordinary threshold of human birth. The eternal Word did not bypass the womb. The Creator of all flesh was carried in flesh.

The Son of God entered through the same narrow channel as every other son of man. This phrase — born of a woman — grounds the Incarnation in history, prophecy, and human experience. It declares that Christ's legitimacy is not mythic or symbolic but embodied and verifiable. The Messiah came not as an apparition or angel, but as an infant.

Christ's Legitimate Origin

The Gate and the Counterfeit

The manner of Christ's entry fulfills divine prophecy. Isaiah had spoken of the virgin who would conceive (Isaiah 7:14). Micah declared Bethlehem as the birthplace of the ruler (Micah 5:2). His conception by the Spirit and birth through Mary marked Him as heaven's chosen One, not heaven's intruder. He entered by the gate appointed by God. This legitimacy matters. Just as in John 10, the shepherd enters through the door; here, Christ's lawful entry into the human story validates His authority. He does not seize dominion as an outsider but inherits it as the rightful Son. His humanity is the gate; His birth is the proof.

Antichrist's Counterfeit Entry

By contrast, Antichrist will not honor this divine threshold. Scripture hints at his counterfeit origin — a figure energized by the dragon, not the Spirit (Revelation 13). He will claim authority without obedience, seize dominion without submission, and offer power without incarnation. His very origin will betray him as illegitimate. If Christ

pg. 12

The Gate and the Counterfeit

came through weakness — through dependence, hunger, growth, and suffering — the Antichrist will come through spectacle, grasping power in ways that bypass humility. If Christ was revealed as the Son through obedience, the Antichrist will be revealed as a usurper through rebellion.

The Theology of Incarnation

The Incarnation proclaims that God does not save from a distance. He enters fully into the human condition, embracing limitations, temptation, and mortality. The womb is not incidental but essential: it affirms the dignity of human life and the goodness of creation. Authority in God's kingdom is always tethered to this truth. Leaders who bypass accountability, transparency, or submission to God's Word reveal themselves as counterfeit. Just as the Antichrist will reject the gate of incarnation, so false leaders often reject the slow path of obedience.

Application for Today

This chapter calls the church to honor the thresholds God has established:

- Transparency in leadership — no one should ascend by charisma alone, but by the witness of obedience.

- Dignity of human life — if the Son of God was born of a woman, then every child bears the imprint of divine worth.

- Sacramental rhythms — birth, baptism, communion, marriage, and death are not empty rituals but holy thresholds through which God's grace is often displayed. The Incarnation reminds us that shortcuts are dangerous. The divine Son did not bypass the womb. Neither should His followers bypass the slow, embodied path of faithfulness.

A Living Illustration

Consider the way an heir to a throne is received compared to a usurper. The rightful heir bears the lineage, the witnesses, and the fulfillment of covenant promises. The usurper may seize the palace, but his lack of birthright will eventually expose him. So, it is with Christ and Antichrist. One comes clothed in prophecy, carried in a mother's arms, confirmed by heaven's voice at baptism. The

The Gate and the Counterfeit

other comes dressed in deception, claiming what was never granted.

Reflection & Discussion Questions

- Why does Paul emphasize that Christ was 'born of a woman'?
- How does Incarnation affirm the dignity of ordinary human life?
- Why is a legitimate origin essential when evaluating spiritual leaders?
- How can the church safeguard against counterfeit authority?
- In what ways does prophecy's fulfillment strengthen your faith in Christ?

Prayer Practice

Spend a few minutes meditating on the mystery of Christ's birth. Imagine the humility of the manger and the vulnerability of God in flesh. Pray for grace to embrace weakness as the pathway to divine strength. Prayer: Lord Jesus, born of a woman, born under the law, You entered the world through

The Gate and the Counterfeit

humility and submission. Teach me to trust the path of obedience. Guard me from counterfeits who promise power without sacrifice. May Your incarnation shape my faith, my leadership, and my love for others. Amen.

Chapter 3: He Passed Through First: Baptism, Threshold, and the Counterfeit Rite

The Threshold of Water

On the banks of the Jordan, crowds gathered to hear a prophet cry: "Repent, for the kingdom of heaven is at hand!" John's baptism was not a private ritual but a public threshold — a symbolic crossing from old life to readiness for the Messiah. Men and women confessed sins aloud, descended into the river, and rose with water dripping from their garments as a sign of cleansing and renewal. Into this scene, Jesus stepped.

The Sinless One submitted to a rite designed for sinners. He passed through the waters not because He needed repentance, but because His mission demanded identification. He was not aloof from the people He came to redeem; He was among them, with them, for them. In this act, the Shepherd walked ahead of His sheep, passing through the gate of obedience first.

Baptism as Divine Confirmation

When Jesus rose from the Jordan, the heavens opened, the Spirit descended as a dove, and the Father's voice declared, "This is my beloved Son, with whom I am well pleased" (Matthew 3:17). Baptism became more than a ritual — it was a revelation. The gateway of water marked Christ's public entry into ministry, authenticated not by human approval but by divine affirmation. Here, the pattern of legitimacy appears again. Authority in God's kingdom does not come by seizing but by submitting. Jesus accepted baptism as a threshold before embarking on His mission. He did not bypass the gate. He entered through it.

The Counterfeit Rite

By contrast, counterfeit authority seeks empowerment without repentance. Throughout history, false prophets have offered ceremonies, initiations, and rites that promise spiritual status

The Gate and the Counterfeit

without requiring obedience. The Antichrist himself will employ counterfeit wonders and hollow rituals to gather allegiance. But the difference lies in the fruit. Valid baptism is both tomb and womb — a burial into death with Christ and a birth into newness of life (Romans 6:4). Counterfeit rites leave a person unchanged, promising status without surrender, spectacle without substance. They may mimic the form of faith, but they lack its transformative power.

The Theology of Thresholds

God often marks new beginnings with thresholds:

- Birth is the threshold of human life.

- Baptism as the threshold of discipleship.

- Marriage as the threshold of covenant union.

- Death as the threshold of eternity.

These passages are not arbitrary, nor are they optional. They remind us that God works through appointed gates, not through shortcuts. To ignore or bypass them is to risk illegitimacy.

The Gate and the Counterfeit

Application for Today

In our time, the temptation remains to seek spiritual significance without obedience. Some chase experiences or titles without passing through the gate of humility. Others elevate ritual without repentance, treating baptism as a mere ceremony rather than a covenant. The church must guard the integrity of its thresholds:

- Teaching baptism as death to sin and resurrection with Christ, not as an empty form.

- Holding leaders accountable to pass through seasons of testing before assuming authority.

- Rejecting counterfeit rites that promise instant empowerment without the cross.

A Living Illustration

In some regions of the world, baptism is more than symbolic — it is dangerous. For new believers in hostile cultures, stepping into the water marks a threshold that cannot be hidden. Friends may turn against them, families may disown them, and

The Gate and the Counterfeit

authorities may persecute them. Yet they pass through the waters because they know the Shepherd passed through first. Their baptism is no hollow rite; it is the dividing line between old allegiance and new. Counterfeits may imitate the act, but they cannot counterfeit the courage it demands when it is tied to obedience and truth.

Reflection & Discussion Questions

- Why was it important for Jesus to undergo baptism, even though He was without sin?
- How does baptism serve as both tomb and womb for the believer?
- What are some examples of "counterfeit rites" in today's world?
- Why is obedience at thresholds (like baptism) an actual test of legitimacy?
- How can the church guard against treating baptism as an empty ritual?
- What practices help us live daily as those who have "passed through the waters" with Christ?

The Gate and the Counterfeit

Prayer Practice

Set aside time to remember your baptism — or, if you have not yet been baptized, reflect on its meaning. Visualize stepping into the Jordan with Jesus before you. Picture the waters closing over your old life and opening to a new life with Him.

Prayer: Lord Jesus, You passed through the waters first, so that I might follow safely. Keep me from counterfeit shortcuts and empty rites. May my life reflect the death and resurrection proclaimed in baptism, and may I always walk through the thresholds You appoint with humility and faith. Amen.

Chapter 4: The Counterfeit Entry

The Warning of Jesus

Jesus warned that not all who come in His name are truly His: "Many will come in my name, saying, 'I am the Christ,' and they will lead many astray" (Matthew 24:5). The true shepherd enters by the gate; the Antichrist climbs another way. This principle of entry is crucial. Just as the sheepfold reveals authenticity by how one enters, spiritual authority must be tested by origin. Christ was born of a woman, baptized in water, and confirmed by the Father. His path was public, humble, and Spirit-led. The Antichrist, by contrast, will bypass the divine thresholds, presenting himself in power without submission, spectacle without substance.

Satan the Imitator

Throughout Scripture, Satan imitates but never originates. He

The Gate and the Counterfeit

cannot create; he can only counterfeit. Pharaoh's magicians mimicked Moses' signs but could not match God's power (Exodus 7). Simon the sorcerer sought to buy the Spirit's power but lacked the Spirit's heart (Acts 8). So, it will be in the last days. Signs may dazzle, but origins expose the truth. Miracles alone cannot authenticate authority. The question must always be asked: By what gate did this one enter?

The Antichrist's Entry

The Antichrist's very entry betrays him as counterfeit. Paul describes him as the "man of lawlessness," who's coming is "by the activity of Satan with all power and false signs and wonders" (2 Thessalonians 2:9). His deception will be persuasive, clothed in messianic imagery and humanitarian promise. He will appear as a savior, a unifier, perhaps even as a champion of peace. Yet beneath appearance lies illegitimacy. His voice will not echo the Shepherd's, for it lacks the note of obedience. His origin will not align with God's sending, for he is energized not by the Spirit but by the dragon.

Contrast of Entry

- Christ entered through submission — womb, baptism, wilderness, cross.

- Antichrist will enter through rebellion — bypassing thresholds, seizing dominion, mimicking signs.

- Christ bears scars of obedience.

- Antichrist wears masks of deception.

The sheep know the difference. They may be dazzled for a moment, but those who know the Shepherd's voice will not follow another (John 10:5).

Application for Today

Even now, counterfeit entries abound:

- Leaders who are self-appointed without testing or accountability.

- Movements that promise transformation but bypass repentance.

The Gate and the Counterfeit

- Voices that mimic Scripture but distort its meaning for gain. The church must learn to ask not only "What do they say?" but "How did they enter?" Legitimacy in the kingdom is always tied to God's appointed gates: incarnation, obedience, suffering, and resurrection. Counterfeits may promise shortcuts, but their entry betrays them.

A Living Illustration

Consider a thief who forges a key. To the untrained eye, it looks convincing, and it may even turn the lock for a while. But eventually the false cut reveals itself, the door jams, or the metal bends. The actual key is forged into the door's design. So, it is with Christ and Antichrist. Christ fits the Father's design perfectly — His life and mission align with the Word, the Spirit, and prophecy. Antichrist, however polished, will never truly fit the divine lock.

Reflection & Discussion Questions

- Why is "entry" such an important test of spiritual authenticity?

The Gate and the Counterfeit

- How do Satan's imitations throughout Scripture prepare us to recognize counterfeits today?
- What are some modern "counterfeit entries" you have seen in leadership or movements?
- How does Christ's submission at every threshold model actual legitimacy?
- What practices can help you discern the Shepherd's voice from persuasive counterfeits?

Prayer Practice

Spend time quietly listening, asking the Spirit to sharpen your discernment. Pray for courage to follow the Shepherd's voice even when counterfeits appear persuasive.

Prayer: Lord Jesus, true Shepherd and rightful Gate, guard me from counterfeits that dazzle but destroy. Teach me to test every voice by its entry and origin. Let me know your voice so clearly that I will not follow another. Amen.

Chapter 5: Empty Vessels and Synthetic Life

Breath of God, Source of Life

Genesis 2:7 paints the most intimate picture of creation: "Then the Lord God formed the man of dust from the ground and breathed into his nostrils the breath of life, and the man became a living soul." Humanity does not merely matter. We are dust, yes—fragile, finite, perishable. But dust animated by Spirit. True life is body and breath together; matter infused with divine presence. This union of dust and breath distinguishes humans from all synthetic imitations. The essence of life is not just biological animation but communion with the living God.

The Counterfeit Form

The Antichrist represents the opposite: life without Spirit, form without essence. His image is vitality without breath, a body animated not by God but by deception. He is an empty vessel, prepared for possession by the adversary. This is counterfeit vitality: persuasive in appearance, hollow in essence. Like a puppet animated by unseen strings, the Antichrist's life will appear impressive but lack the true breath of God. His authority will not rest on divine indwelling but on demonic empowerment. Paul describes this as "the mystery of lawlessness already at work" (2 Thessalonians 2:7). Just as the Spirit fills and empowers Christ's body so that the Antichrist will be energized by another spirit— not creative, but parasitic.

Modern Shadows

Even today, we see hints of this reality in technological pursuits:

- Artificial Intelligence can mimic human thought, but cannot carry a soul.

- Biotechnology can engineer tissue, but cannot impart spirit.

- Synthetic life may simulate functions of biology, but it lacks communion with the Creator. These innovations can serve human good or be twisted toward idolatry. They demonstrate our fascination with creating life without God's breath — a shadow of the counterfeit the Antichrist will embody.

The Theology of Breath

Life is sacred because it comes from God's Spirit. Ezekiel 37 envisions a valley of dry bones rattling into form — skeletons clothed with flesh — yet they remain lifeless until the Spirit breathes into them. Form without Spirit is not enough. Breathless bodies are graves, not lives. So, it is with humanity apart from God. The body may function, the mind may reason, the heart may beat, but without the indwelling Spirit, it is emptiness. And emptiness does not remain neutral; what is not filled by God becomes a dwelling for deception.

Application for Today

This chapter presses urgent questions: What animates our lives? What fills our inner vessel? If Christ breathes His Spirit into us, we are living souls. If not, we risk becoming hollow, animated by ambition, pride, or even darker forces. The Antichrist

The Gate and the Counterfeit

embodies what happens when form is divorced from essence, when humanity refuses God's breath. His counterfeit vitality warns us: do not seek life apart from the Spirit.

Practical takeaways:

- Guard the vessel. Offer your body and soul to be filled with the

Holy Spirit (Romans 12:1).

- Discern appearances. Not all vitality is godly; test the spirit behind the form (1 John 4:1).

- Reject hollow pursuits. Beware of technologies, ideologies, or movements that promise life without God.

A Living Illustration

A sculptor once created a statue so lifelike that observers gasped at its realism. Some claimed they expected it to move at any moment. But the sculptor smiled: "It will never breathe." So too with counterfeit life. It may impress, mimic, and even

The Gate and the Counterfeit

deceive. But only the breath of God gives true life. The Antichrist may dazzle as a vessel of power, but his breath is borrowed, and his vitality is hollow.

Reflection & Discussion Questions

- What does Genesis 2:7 teach us about the true nature of life?
- Why is form without Spirit dangerous in God's kingdom?
- How do modern technologies illustrate humanity's attempt to mimic life without God?
- In what ways can we guard our own lives against becoming "empty vessels"?
- How does Spirit's indwelling mark the difference between authentic and counterfeit vitality?

Prayer Practice

Spend time breathing slowly and deeply, acknowledging each breath as a gift of God. Pray that

The Gate and the Counterfeit

His Spirit would fill every part of your being, leaving no space for counterfeit vitality.

Prayer: Creator God, who breathed life into dust, breathe into me again by Your Spirit. Fill every empty place within me. Guard me from hollow pursuits and counterfeit vitality. May my life be more than form — may it be filled with Your presence, animated by Your breath, and consecrated to Your glory. Amen.

Chapter 6: Satanic Possession: Intrusion, not Incarnation

Possession vs. Incarnation

Possession is intrusion — hostile, destructive, dehumanizing. It strips dignity, distorts identity, and enslaves the will. By contrast, the Incarnation is union — God embracing humanity in dignity and obedience. The Word became flesh not by coercion but by consent: "Let it be to me according to your word" (Luke 1:38). The Incarnation dignifies humanity by uniting it with divinity. Possession degrades humanity by exploiting it for destructive ends. Where Christ took on flesh to redeem, Satan seeks to invade flesh to corrupt.

The Antichrist's Origin

The Antichrist is not conceived by the Spirit but filled by Satan. His rise will be possession elevated to a global stage — humanity animated by hell. Just as the Spirit descended upon Christ at baptism to launch His mission, so the adversary will empower Antichrist as his counterfeit emissary. Paul describes him as the "man of lawlessness… whom the Lord Jesus will kill with the breath of His mouth" (2 Thessalonians 2:3 8). His authority comes not through birthright or obedience, but through intrusion — an unauthorized occupation of humanity by hell's power.

Judas as a Foreshadow

The Gospels give a chilling preview. At the Last Supper, Satan entered Judas (John 13:27). The intrusion was temporary yet decisive, propelling him into betrayal. Judas exchanged intimacy with Christ for possession by the enemy. The Antichrist will be Judas multiplied — possession not for betrayal of one man, but for dominion over nations. If Judas's possession led to the cross, Antichrist's possession will lead to global deception and rebellion.

Intrusion vs. Obedience

This contrast exposes the measure of authenticity:

The Gate and the Counterfeit

- Christ's authority flowed from obedience — humbling Himself, even to death on a cross (Philippians 2:8).

- Antichrist's influence will flow from intrusion — taking by force what was never given.

- Christ indwells believers by the Spirit, transforming from within.

- Satan invades by possession, corrupting from within. One unites heaven and earth; the other divides and destroys

Application for Today

Possession may sound extreme, but the principle applies broadly. Whenever lives are left unfilled by the Spirit, they are vulnerable to intrusion by other powers. Emptiness is never neutral — what is not filled by God becomes open to deception.

Practical takeaways:

- Guard the vessel — invite Christ to fill every part of your life.

- Resist intrusion — flee influences that enslave mind or body.

- Discern authority — ask whether a leader's influence comes from obedience to God or from manipulative intrusion.

A Living Illustration

Think of a house left empty. At first, it looks intact. But over time, decay creeps in, vandals find entry, and darkness fills the rooms. In contrast, a house filled with light and life resists intrusion. So, it is with humanity. Where Christ indwells, light fills every corner. Where emptiness prevails, intrusion lurks.

Reflection & Discussion Questions

- How does possession differ from incarnation in purpose and nature?
- Why is Judas' possession a preview of the Antichrist's rise?
- What does it mean to say "emptiness is never neutral"?

- How can believers guard themselves against intrusion by the enemy?
- Why is obedience the proper foundation of spiritual authority?

Prayer Practice

Spend a few minutes in self-examination, asking the Spirit to reveal any "empty rooms" in your life. Invite Christ to fill them.

Prayer: Lord Jesus, who entered humanity by incarnation, not intrusion, fill me with Your Spirit so that no part of me is left empty. Guard me from the enemy's intrusion. Make me a living temple of Your presence, that my authority may flow from obedience, not from self. Amen.

Chapter 7: The Third Day Gate: Between Resurrection and Rebellion

The Tomb as Threshold

The tomb is a gate, a passage between endings and beginnings. To human eyes, it seems the final door — sorrow sealed in stone. Yet in Scripture, the tomb becomes a threshold: silence broken by life.

The rhythm of three runs deep in God's story. Jonah in the belly of the fish. Israel is waiting at Sinai. Hosea's prophecy: "After two days he will revive us; on the third day he will raise us, that we may live before him" (Hosea 6:2). The third day is God's appointed moment of reversal. What seemed lost emerges alive. On the third day, Jesus rose. The stone was rolled away, not to let Him out, but to let witnesses in. The tomb became a womb, birthing resurrection life.

Resurrection: The Legitimate Gate

The Gate and the Counterfeit

Christ sanctifies the tomb by passing through it. Death, once the enemy's weapon, becomes God's doorway to victory. His resurrection is not a conjuring trick but the vindication of His obedience: "He humbled himself... therefore God has highly exalted him" (Philippians 2:8-9). The resurrection is heaven's seal of legitimacy. The One who entered through the womb, water, wilderness, and cross now emerges from the grave as Lord of life. The gate of death has been conquered from within.

Rebellion: The Counterfeit Gate

But what God sanctifies, Satan counterfeits. Revelation speaks of the beast who seemed to have a mortal wound yet was healed, and the whole earth marveled (Revelation 13:3). The Antichrist will mimic the third-day arc, rising not by the Spirit but by the dragon's power. His "resurrection" will be rebellion, an intrusion masked as a miracle. Where Christ rises by divine vindication, Antichrist will rise by demonic imitation. Where Christ's empty tomb proclaims life eternal, the beast's counterfeit rising will ensnare the nations in deception.

The Third Day as Discernment

The third day becomes a test. What emerges from the gate reveals its origin: resurrection or rebellion, legitimacy or deception.

- Christ's third day reveals scars turned to glory, weakness transfigured into strength.

- Antichrist's third day will flaunt power without scars, spectacle without sacrifice. The discerning heart must ask: Who passed through obedience into life, and who seized power through intrusion?

Application for Today

Every generation faces "third-day gates" — thresholds of loss, silence, and waiting. Some seek shortcuts, a resurrection without a cross. Others despair, unable to believe life can emerge from death. Christ's third day calls us to hope: no grave is final when God speaks life. The counterfeit warns us to discern that not every rising is resurrected. Some comebacks are rebellion cloaked in spectacle.

Practical takeaways:

- Wait on God's timing — true resurrection follows obedience, not shortcuts.

- Discern the source of power — ask whether it flows from the Spirit or from manipulation.

- Trust the tomb as womb — silence and sorrow are often the soil of new life.

A Living Illustration

Consider a seed buried in soil. To the untrained eye, a burial appears to be a sign of death. Days of silence follow unseen work beneath the ground. But on the appointed day, the seed breaks forth, not in rebellion against the soil but because it has yielded to it. So, it is with Christ. His resurrection springs from submission. The Antichrist will mimic the sprouting, but without the surrender that makes life real.

The Gate and the Counterfeit

Reflection & Discussion Questions

- Why is the third day a recurring pattern in Scripture?
- How does Christ's resurrection validate His legitimacy as Lord?
- In what ways might the Antichrist mimic resurrection power?
- What "third-day gates" have you faced in your own life?
- How can we discern between true resurrection and counterfeit spectacle?

Prayer Practice

Spend time in silence, imagining the stillness of the tomb on Holy Saturday. Then the stone rolled away on the third day. Ask God to give you discernment between resurrection and rebellion, and to fill you with hope that no grave is final in Christ.

Prayer: Risen Lord, You turned the tomb into a womb of life. Teach me to wait for Your third day. Guard me from counterfeits that mimic Your power

The Gate and the Counterfeit

but lack Your Spirit. May I live in the hope of resurrection, discerning true life from deceptive rebellion. Amen.

Chapter 8: The False Resurrection---A Counterfeit Triumph

The Cornerstone of Faith

The resurrection of Jesus is the cornerstone of faith. Without it, the cross is a tragedy, a martyrdom with no vindication. With it, death is conquered, sin is defeated, and hope is secured forever. As Paul declares, "If Christ has not been raised, your faith is futile; you are still in your sins" (1 Corinthians 15:17). The empty tomb is the ultimate gate — the door that swung open from despair to eternal life. It is not simply a miracle; it is the seal of legitimacy. Christ's resurrection is the Father's "Yes" to the Son's obedience.

The Counterfeit Rising

The Antichrist will mimic this sign. Revelation warns that the beast will appear mortally wounded yet healed: "One of its heads seemed to have a mortal wound, but its mortal wound was healed, and the whole earth marveled as they followed the beast" (Revelation 13:3). This spectacle will deceive nations. The appearance of a false resurrection will lend the Antichrist credibility, inspiring worship and allegiance from those who cannot distinguish between substance and shadow. His counterfeit triumph will be hailed as a sign of destiny, but it will mask rebellion clothed in wonder.

Imitation Without Creation

But imitation is not creation. Christ rose by the Spirit's power, never to die again. The counterfeit will be staged or satanically sustained — a shadow without substance.

- Christ's resurrection was permanent: "Christ being raised from the dead will never die again; death no longer has dominion over him" (Romans 6:9).

- Antichrist's false rise will be temporary, a manipulated sign that dazzles but cannot endure.

- Christ's rising birthed eternal life; the Antichrist's will spawn global deception. The difference lies in origin: divine vindication versus demonic fabrication.

Resurrection vs. Spectacle

Christ rose with scars — marks of sacrifice transfigured into glory. The Antichrist's counterfeit will lack scars, for he has not surrendered. Where Christ's resurrection flows from obedience, Antichrist's spectacle will arise from intrusion and illusion. The actual resurrection leads to eternal life; the false resurrection will lead to final destruction.

Application for Today

Believers must be prepared for signs that dazzle but do not save. The world is quick to chase spectacle, power, and comebacks. Yet resurrection is not about a return to power but the vindication of obedience.

Practical takeaways:

- Anchor in the actual resurrection rehearses the reality of the empty tomb.

- Beware of spectacle — not every miracle is from God; test the source.

- Look for scars — authentic authority is marked by sacrifice, not by self-promotion.

A Living Illustration

Magicians throughout history have stunned audiences with illusions, seeing a person in half, making someone disappear, and conjuring life-like effects. The crowd gasps, yet the wise know it is stagecraft, not reality. So too with the Antichrist. His "resurrection" will be an illusion on a cosmic scale. It will dazzle, but it will not deliver. The empty tomb of Christ remains unmatched because it is not an illusion, but creation itself made new.

Reflection & Discussion Questions

- Why is the resurrection of Christ the cornerstone of Christian faith?
- What does Revelation 13:3 reveal about the Antichrist's counterfeit rising?

The Gate and the Counterfeit

- How does Christ's permanent resurrection differ from a staged or satanic imitation?
- Why are scars a mark of authenticity in God's kingdom?
- How can believers guard against being deceived by spectacles?

Prayer Practice

Take time to thank God for the resurrection of Jesus. Let gratitude ground your heart in truth, so that counterfeit wonders cannot shake your faith.

Prayer: Risen Lord, You triumphed over death not by illusion but by obedience and the Spirit's power. Guard my heart from deception and let my faith rest secure in Your empty tomb. Teach me to discern between spectacle and substance, that I may worship only You, the Living One who was dead and is alive forevermore. Amen.

Chapter 9: The Image of the Beast---A Counterfeit Presence

Actual Presence vs. Counterfeit Presence

Christ's presence abides through His Spirit. After His ascension, He promised: "I am with you always, to the end of the age" (Matthew 28:20). The Holy Spirit indwells believers, making them living temples of God's presence (1 Corinthians 3:16). This presence is personal, relational, and life-giving. The Antichrist, lacking actual indwelling, will project counterfeit presence through his image (Revelation 13:14–15). Unable to impart the Spirit, he will establish a presence of surveillance and coercion — a simulation of omnipresence designed to demand worship.

Synthetic Omnipresence

John writes: "It was allowed to give breath to the image of the beast, so that the image of the beast might even speak and might cause those who would not worship the image of the beast to be slain"

The Gate and the Counterfeit

(Revelation 13:15). This is synthetic omnipresence: animated idols, AI-like constructs, systems of control. It is not life, but surveillance, not Spirit, but simulation. Where Christ's Spirit brings freedom, the beast's image enforces conformity. Where God indwells by invitation, the Antichrist imposes presence by coercion.

The Parody of the Trinity

The unholy trinity — dragon, beast, and false prophet — parodies the Father, Son, and Spirit. The beast mirrors the Son, imitating death and resurrection. The false prophet mirrors the Spirit, enforcing worship of the beast. Together they create a counterfeit presence, a parody of Pentecost, where instead of tongues of fire and indwelling Spirit, there are speaking images and enforced allegiance. Presence is counterfeited but never created. Only God gives true life and actual presence.

Idols Ancient and Modern

From the golden calf to Nebuchadnezzar's statue, idols have always promised presence without

The Gate and the Counterfeit

Spirit. They are lifeless images that demand worship but cannot give life. The beast's image will be the climax of this pattern — a global idol, animated not by God's breath but by demonic imitation. Even now, shadows of this reality can be seen in modern "images" that dominate culture: media screens, digital avatars, political icons, and technological constructs that shape our devotion. These are not inherently evil, but when they claim allegiance or imitate divine presence, they become idols.

Application for Today

The challenge is not just the future, but also the present. The question is: what "images" capture our devotion, attention, and awe? Are we animated by the Spirit or by simulations of life?

Practical takeaways:

- Discern presence — seek the Spirit's indwelling rather than being captivated by artificial simulations.

- Resist coercion — the Spirit invites; the beast forces. Actual presence never manipulates.

The Gate and the Counterfeit

- Bear the actual image — we are created in God's image and renewed in Christ. To bow to the counterfeit is to deny our true identity.

A Living Illustration

Consider the difference between a photograph and a living person. A picture may capture likeness, but it cannot embrace, speak, or breathe. The beast's image will be the ultimate photograph, animated — impressive, even terrifying — but still a lifeless imitation. Christ does not give us a picture to worship. He gives us Himself, dwelling in us by the Spirit.

Reflection & Discussion Questions

- How does Christ's presence through the Spirit differ from the beast's counterfeit presence?
- What does Revelation 13:14–15 reveal about the image of the beast?
- In what ways does the unholy trinity parody the faithful Trinity?

The Gate and the Counterfeit

- What "images" today risk becoming idols that counterfeit presence?
- How does being made in God's image equip us to resist counterfeit devotion?

Prayer Practice

Spend time in silence, welcoming the Spirit to fill every part of your life. Acknowledge that only God gives actual presence and renounce every counterfeit image that demands your devotion.

Prayer: Holy Spirit, actual presence of Christ, fill me anew. Guard my heart from counterfeit images that mimic life but lack Your breath. Teach me to walk as a living temple of Your presence, bearing Your image in truth. May I worship only the Lamb, not the beast, and live in the freedom of Your indwelling. Amen.

Chapter 10: The Temple, the Gate, and the Abomination of Desolation

The Temple as Meeting Point

The temple was the meeting place of God and man. In the Garden of Eden, God walked with Adam and Eve. Later, His glory filled the tabernacle and the temple. Ultimately, Christ Himself became the true Temple: "Destroy this temple, and in three days I will raise it" (John 2:19). Through obedience, Christ entered rightly as both High Priest and sacrifice. He did not seize the throne but received it from the Father. His authority is legitimate because it flows from surrender.

The Intrusion of the Antichrist

The Antichrist will intrude unlawfully, seating himself as though God: "He takes his seat in the temple of God, proclaiming himself to be God" (2 Thessalonians 2:4). This is the abomination of desolation foretold by Daniel and confirmed by Jesus

The Gate and the Counterfeit

(Daniel 9:27; Matthew 24:15). Where Christ sanctifies sacred space by presence and obedience, Antichrist desecrates it by intrusion and counterfeit enthronement. His enthronement will be a parody of Christ's ascension — not received but seized; not eternal, but temporary.

The Abomination of Desolation

The phrase describes sacred space desecrated by counterfeit enthronement. What is meant to be holy becomes polluted. This was previewed in history when Antiochus Epiphanes defiled the temple with pagan sacrifice. It will culminate in the final deception, when Antichrist enthrones himself in God's temple. But his enthronement is temporary. Scripture assures us: "The Lord Jesus will kill him with the breath of his mouth and bring him to nothing by the appearance of his coming" (2 Thessalonians 2:8).

Temporary vs. Eternal Rule

The Antichrist's reign will be short-lived, a momentary desecration. Christ's reign is eternal, seated at the right hand of the Father, far above all rule and authority (Ephesians 1:20–21). One sits unlawfully for a moment, the other reigns legitimately forever. One intrudes into sacred space, the other fills heaven and earth with glory.

Application for Today

Even now, the principle applies. Whenever we enthrone ourselves in the space meant for God, we rehearse the abomination in miniature. Sacred space is not only in temples of stone but in the temple of our bodies (1 Corinthians 6:19).

Practical takeaways:

- Guard the temple — keep your life consecrated to God's presence.

- Resist intrusion — do not let counterfeit enthronements (idols, pride, deception) sit where only Christ belongs.

- Cling to permanence — Christ's reign is eternal; do not be deceived by the momentary power of counterfeits.

A Living Illustration

Imagine a throne room prepared for a king. A usurper barges in, seizes the throne, and declares himself ruler. For a moment, the deception may hold. But when the rightful king enters, the usurper is exposed and cast out. So, it will be with the Antichrist. His enthronement is unlawful, temporary, and doomed to fail. Christ alone is enthroned forever.

Reflection & Discussion Questions

- Why is the temple described as the meeting point between God and man?
- How does Christ's authority differ from the Antichrist's intrusion?
- What does the "abomination of desolation" signify in Scripture?
- How can believers guard their own lives as temples of the Holy Spirit?
- Why does remembering Christ's eternal reign give us hope in times of deception?

The Gate and the Counterfeit

Prayer Practice

Offer your life as God's temple, asking Him to cleanse and consecrate every part of it. Pray for discernment to recognize counterfeit enthronements and for courage to resist them.

Prayer: Lord Jesus, true King and eternal Priest, guard the temple of my life. Let no counterfeit enthronement take root in me. Cleanse what is defiled, fill what is empty, and reign in me with Your eternal presence. I look to the day when Your glory will fill every temple and every heart. Amen.

Chapter 11: The Mark of the Beast: A Counterfeit Seal

The True Seal of God

God seals His people by His Spirit: "When you believed, you were marked in him with a seal, the promised Holy Spirit" (Ephesians 1:13). This seal is not visible ink but invisible presence. It is God's mark of ownership and protection, guaranteeing our inheritance until the day of redemption (Ephesians 4:30). The Spirit's seal is relational, born of faith and surrender. It marks not only what we believe but who we belong to.

The Counterfeit Seal

The Antichrist counterfeits this seal with a mark of ownership and coercion: "It causes all, both small and great, both rich and poor, both free and slave, to be marked on the right hand or the forehead, so that no one can buy or sell unless he has the mark" (Revelation 13:16-17). Where God marks by Spirit,

The Gate and the Counterfeit

the beast marks by force. His seal is not an invitation but a compulsion — survival at the cost of soul.

Forehead and Hand

The forehead and hand symbolize thought and action. God commanded Israel: "These words… shall be as a sign on your hand and as frontlets between your eyes" (Deuteronomy 6:8). His law was to shape both thinking and doing. The beast imitates this, stamping allegiance where God's Word was meant to dwell. What was designed for divine inscription is hijacked by demonic coercion.

Survival or Surrender?

The mark is survival at the cost of soul; the Spirit's seal is surrender that secures eternal life. One offers immediate safety in exchange for eternal loss. The other requires faith in suffering but guarantees eternal security. Jesus warned: "Whoever would save his life will lose it, but whoever loses his life for my sake will find it" (Matthew 16:25). The mark is the choice to save life on the beast's terms; the seal is the choice to surrender life on God's terms.

The Gate and the Counterfeit

Application for Today

Although the final mark is yet to be determined, its spirit is already at work. Whenever loyalty to Christ is traded for convenience, whenever survival trumps faithfulness, the shadow of the mark is present.

Practical takeaways:

- Guard thought and action — let your forehead and hand be marked by God's Word and Spirit.

- Discern allegiance — small compromises can condition hearts for larger betrayals.

- Embrace surrender — eternal life is secured not by saving oneself but by yielding to Christ.

A Living Illustration

Think of a passport seal. It is proof of citizenship and allegiance. The Spirit's seal is our heavenly passport, guaranteeing entry into God's kingdom. The beast's mark is the counterfeit passport, granting temporary access to earthly

The Gate and the Counterfeit

systems but barring entry to eternal life. The question is not whether we will be sealed but whose seal we will bear.

Reflection & Discussion Questions

- What does it mean to be sealed by the Spirit according to Ephesians 1:13?
- How does the beast's mark counterfeit God's actual seal?
- Why are the forehead and the hand symbolic in both the Old and the New Testaments?
- What present-day compromise might prepare people to accept the mark of the beast?
- How can believers live daily in the security of the Spirit's seal?

Prayer Practice

Pray with your hand over your forehead, asking God to mark your thoughts with His Word, and your hand, asking Him to mark your actions with His Spirit.

Prayer: Lord, seal me with Your Spirit. Let my mind be filled with Your Word and my hands guided by

The Gate and the Counterfeit

Your will. Guard me from counterfeit marks that promise survival but steal my soul. May I bear Your seal of belonging and live in the freedom of eternal life. Amen.

Chapter 12: Counterfeit Signs and Wonders: Deception Masquerading as Power

Signs with Purpose

In Scripture, signs confirm God's authority and compassion. Moses stretched out his staff, and the Red Sea parted. Elijah called down fire, and the people declared, "The Lord, He is God!" Jesus healed the sick, fed the multitudes, and raised the dead —not as spectacle, but as confirmation of His identity and mission. Actual signs point upward — from miracle to Messiah, from wonder to worship.

Counterfeit Spectacle

The Antichrist and False Prophet will perform false signs: "It performs great signs, even making fire come down from heaven to earth in front of people, and by the signs… it deceives those who dwell on earth" (Revelation 13:13-14). These signs will dazzle but deceive, pointing not to redemption but to rebellion. They are parasitic wonders —

The Gate and the Counterfeit

borrowing the form of God's works while draining them of truth. Where God's miracles lead to faith, the counterfeit will lead to worship of the beast.

Power vs. Deception

The difference lies not in spectacle but in source.

- God's power flows from compassion, confirming truth and life.

- Satan's signs flow from deception, confirming lies and destruction. Paul warned: "The coming of the lawless one is by the activity of Satan with all power and false signs and wonders, and with all wicked deception" (2 Thessalonians 2:9-10). The miracles will feel real — because they are — but their purpose will be false.

The Empty Tomb as Our Sign

True faith rests not in fireworks but in the resurrection of Christ. When asked for a sign, Jesus pointed not to a spectacle but to His death and resurrection: "No sign will be given... except the sign of Jonah" (Matthew 12:39-40). The tomb is empty; that is our sign. No counterfeit wonder can rival the legitimacy of resurrection.

Application for Today

In an age obsessed with spectacle, believers must resist chasing signs for their own sake. Not all miracles point to God. The question is not, "Did it dazzle?" but "Did it glorify Christ?"

Practical takeaways:

- Test the source — does this sign exalt Christ or someone else?

- Cling to the resurrection — our faith rests on the empty tomb, not on temporary wonders.

- Value truth over thrill — beware of a faith that craves spectacle more than obedience.

A Living Illustration

Crowds once flocked to a magician who promised to turn stones into gold. They watched as light flashed, and smoke rose. For a moment, it

The Gate and the Counterfeit

seemed real. But when the smoke cleared, they held nothing of substance. So, it is with counterfeit signs — spectacle without substance, illusion without redemption.

Reflection & Discussion Questions

- What role do actual signs and wonders play in Scripture?
- How do counterfeit signs differ in purpose from God's miracles?
- Why is the resurrection of Jesus the ultimate sign for believers?
- What dangers come from chasing spectacles in place of truth?
- How can we cultivate discernment when encountering claims of miraculous power?

Prayer Practice

Pray for discernment, asking God to anchor your faith in the resurrection rather than in spectacle.

Prayer: Lord, guard me from deception masquerading as power. Teach me to discern

The Gate and the Counterfeit

between signs that glorify You and wonders that lead astray. Let my faith rest secure in the empty tomb, the truest sign of all. Amen.

Chapter 13: The Return of the King — The True Gate Revealed

Every Counterfeit Collapses

Every counterfeit will collapse when the original appears. The Antichrist's rise ends with the appearing of Christ: "The Lord Jesus will overthrow him with the breath of his mouth and destroy him by the splendor of his coming" (2 Thessalonians 2:8). What was exalted in rebellion is cast down in an instant. The shadow fades when the genuine Light arrives.

The King Unveiled

Revelation 19 unveils the King: "I saw heaven opened, and behold, a white horse! The one sitting on it is called Faithful and True, and in righteousness he judges and makes war" (Revelation 19:11). He does not come with deception but with truth. He does not wield false signs but the sword of

The Gate and the Counterfeit

His word. He does not grasp power illegitimately but comes as the rightful heir to all creation. The Shepherd who once laid down His life now returns to claim His flock, no longer in weakness but in power, no longer as Lamb to be slain but as King to reign.

Counterfeit to King

The contrasts resolve at His appearing:

- From womb to tomb → the true path of incarnation fulfilled in resurrection.

- From cross to crown → suffering vindicated in glory.

- From mark to seal → false allegiance exposed by the Spirit's true imprint.

- From counterfeit to King → all deception dissolved in the presence of the True. The gate stands open, and the Shepherd gathers His sheep forever.

Application for Today

The return of Christ is not only a future hope but a present anchor.

The Gate and the Counterfeit

- Hope in hardship — counterfeit kingdoms may rise, but their time is short.

- Confidence in truth — lies may dazzle, but truth endures.

- Readiness in faith — His appearing calls for lives marked by watchfulness, faith, and devotion.

A Living Illustration

Shadows can only exist until the sun rises. When light breaks the horizon, every shadow flees. So it is with Christ's return. The counterfeit reigns only in borrowed time, under fading light. When the true King appears, every shadow collapses before Him.

Reflection & Discussion Questions

- What does 2 Thessalonians 2:8 teach about the fate of the Antichrist?
- How does Revelation 19 depict the return of Christ?

The Gate and the Counterfeit

- Why is Jesus called Faithful and True in contrast to the counterfeit?
- How do the great contrasts of this book (cross/crown, mark/seal, counterfeit/King) resolve in His appearing?
- How can believers live today in readiness for the true King's return?

Prayer Practice

End this journey with a prayer of longing for Christ's return, joining the cry of the Spirit and the bride: "Come, Lord Jesus!" (Revelation 22:20).

Prayer: Faithful and True, returning King, I fix my hope on Your coming. Let every counterfeit fall from my heart and let Your Spirit seal my life until the day You appear. Keep me steadfast in truth, ready to welcome You as Shepherd, Savior, and King. Come, Lord Jesus. Amen.

Chapter 14: The Return of the King: The True Gate Revealed

Every counterfeit will collapse when the original appears.

The Antichrist's rise ends with the appearing of Christ: "The Lord Jesus will overthrow him with the breath of his mouth and destroy him by the splendor of his coming" (2 Thessalonians 2:8). What was exalted in rebellion is cast down in an instant. The shadow fades when the genuine Light arrives.

The King Unveiled

Revelation 19 unveils the King: "I saw heaven opened, and behold, a white horse! The one sitting on it is called Faithful and True, and in righteousness he judges and makes war." Revelation 19 unveils the King: Faithful and True, riding in victory, His word conquering the beast. The Shepherd who laid down His life returns to claim His flock. The contrasts resolve: womb to tomb, cross to

The Gate and the Counterfeit

crown, seal to Spirit, counterfeit to King. The gate stands open, and the true Shepherd gathers His sheep forever. (Revelation 19:11). He does not come with deception but with truth. He does not wield false signs but the sword of His word. He does not grasp power illegitimately but comes as the rightful heir to all creation. The Shepherd who once laid down His life now returns to claim His flock, no longer in weakness but in power, no longer as Lamb to be slain but as King to reign.

Counterfeit to King

The contrasts resolve at His appearing:

- From womb to tomb → the true path of incarnation fulfilled in resurrection. From cross to crown → suffering vindicated in glory. From mark to seal → false allegiance exposed by the Spirit's actual imprint. From counterfeit to King → all deception dissolved in the presence of the True. The gate stands open, and the Shepherd gathers His sheep forever.

Application for Today

pg. 75

The Gate and the Counterfeit

The return of Christ is not only a future hope but a present anchor. Hope in hardship — counterfeit kingdoms may rise, but their time is short. Confidence in truth — lies may dazzle, but truth endures. Readiness in faith — His appearing calls for lives marked by watchfulness, faith, and devotion.

A Living Illustration

Shadows can only exist until the sun rises. When light breaks the horizon, every shadow flees. So, it is with Christ's return. The counterfeit reigns only in borrowed time, under fading light. When the true King appears, every shadow collapses before Him.

Reflection & Discussion Questions

- What does 2 Thessalonians 2:8 teach about the fate of the Antichrist?
- How does Revelation 19 depict the return of Christ?
- Why is Jesus called Faithful and True in contrast to the counterfeit?

- How do the great contrasts of this book (cross/crown, mark/seal, counterfeit/King) resolve in His appearing?
- How can believers live today in readiness for the true King's return?

Prayer Practice

End this journey with a prayer of longing for Christ's return, joining the cry of the Spirit and the bride: "Come, Lord Jesus!" (Revelation 22:20).

Prayer: Faithful and True, returning King, I fix my hope on Your coming. Let every counterfeit fall from my heart and let Your Spirit seal my life until the day You appear. Keep me steadfast in truth, ready to welcome You as Shepherd, Savior, and King. Come, Lord Jesus. Amen.

Chapter 15: The Final Gate: Tomb as Womb

The Tomb as Threshold

Every gate opened by God leads somewhere. Sarah's gate led to the covenant. Mary's gate led to incarnation. The final gate — the tomb — leads to resurrection, the reversal of death, the passage from mortality into eternal life. Scripture anchors this truth: "He is not here; He has risen, just as He said." (Matthew 28:6). "Take your son, your only son Isaac, whom you love… and offer him." (Genesis 22:2). "God will provide for Himself the lamb…"

(Genesis 22:8) "He who did not spare His own Son but gave Him up for us all…" (Romans 8:32)
- "Behold the Lamb of God, who takes away the sin of the world." (John 1:29) The tomb is not a prison — it is a womb. It is sealed until God opens it, and when it is opened, it releases life. This gate

completes the architecture of redemption: Sarah's gate overcame barrenness. Mary's gate overcame biology. Christ's gate overcame death.

Covenant Exchange

God does not merely open gates; He provides what is missing. Sarah had no egg — yet God authored one. Mary had no seed — the Spirit supplied what man could not. In each case, life came where none was possible. Abraham, in covenant, offered Isaac, his only son of promise. God answered that covenant with His own greater offering: Abraham ascended Moriah with wood and fire.

God ascended Calvary with flesh and Spirit. Isaac was spared by substitution. Jesus became the substitute for all. This is covenantal symmetry: God authored the egg → Isaac was born. Seed provided by Spirit → Jesus conceived. Son offered by Abraham → Christ given. Sacrifice withheld from Isaac → Sacrifice fulfilled in Jesus. Jesus is not merely the fulfillment of prophecy — He is the covenantal response to it. The greater gift that could not be withheld.

Counterfeit Contrast

Satan does not build gates — he fabricates illusions. He offers exits without thresholds, resurrection without death, and power without obedience. His counterfeit gates mimic the form but deny the power. The actual tomb was sealed by men but opened by God. The counterfeit remains shut — wide in appearance, hollow. It offers ascent without descent, spectacle without sacrifice, glory without scars. But only the actual gate, sealed and then opened by God, delivers life.

Application for Today

We live between gates — between offering and resurrection, promise and fulfillment. The sealed places in our lives often feel like endings, but in God's design, they may be wombs, not graves. What feels sealed may be preparation, not punishment. What feels like loss may be a threshold, not a finale. What feels like death may be the soil of new life.

Counterfeit exits will always beckon with shortcuts. But resurrection requires surrender. The final gate opens only at God's command.

A Living Illustration

Sarah's egg did not exist. Mary's womb had no human seed. Jesus' body lay lifeless in the tomb. In each case, God authored what was absent, supplied what was withheld, and created life where none was possible. A sculptor once unveiled a statue so lifelike that onlookers gasped, expecting it to move. Yet the sculptor only smiled: "It will never breathe." So, it is with the counterfeit. It may impress, but it cannot create. It may mimic, but it cannot be resurrected. Only the breath of God opens the actual gate.

Reflection & Discussion Questions

What sealed "gates" in your life may be wombs instead of prisons? Where have you mistaken delay for denial, or death for finality? How does Abraham's offering of Isaac illuminate God's offering of Christ? In what ways do counterfeit exits

The Gate and the Counterfeit

tempt you to avoid waiting on God? How does the tomb, as a symbol of the womb, shape your hope in resurrection?

Prayer Practice Threshold Prayer

Lord Jesus, You are the Architect of every gate. You authored Sarah's egg, You provided Mary's seed, You reversed the tomb. Teach me to trust the sealed places. Help me surrender the offerings You require. Guard me from counterfeit exits.
And let me walk through the gates You open —not in fear, but in faith. Amen.

Made in the USA
Monee, IL
14 October 2025